A New True Book

UNITED NATIONS

By Carol Greene

This "true book" was prepared
under the direction of
Illa Podendorf,
formerly with the Laboratory School,
University of Chicago

CHILDRENS PRESS, CHICAGO

PHOTO CREDITS

UNICEF—2, 27 (right), 30 (2 photos), 31, 40, 41

Mark Rosenthal—27 (left), 36 (left)

Chandler Forman—33, 36 (right), 37, 43, (3 photos), 45

Hillstrom Stock Photos—©Jack Lund, 4 (2 photos)

Karen Jacobsen—35

United Nations—Photographs and Exhibits Section, Office of Public Information—Cover, 7, 8, 12, 15, 17, 18 (right), 23, 24, 44

UN Photo Library—11, 18 (left)

Associated Press—20 (2 photos), 38

World Health Organization (WHO)—28 (2 photos), 29 (2 photos)

COVER—The General Assembly

Young girl from Sri Lanka with the UNICEF symbol in the lower right corner. The UNICEF fund is devoted to helping children.

***This book is for
all the children UNICEF helps,
for all the children who help UNICEF,
and
for Janet Roberts.***

Library of Congress Cataloging in Publication Data

Greene, Carol.
    The United Nations.

    (A New true book)
    Includes index.
Summary: An introduction to the United Nations describing its purpose and organization and the work of its many specialized agencies.
    1. United Nations—Juvenile literature. [1. United Nations] I. Title. II. Series.
JX1977.Z8G73 1983   341.23   83-10068
ISBN 0-516-01710-1   AACR2

TABLE OF CONTENTS

People of Leningrad, USSR (above) and Nazare, Portugal (below).
Both countries belong to the United Nations.

ONE BIG FAMILY

What if all the countries in the world belonged to one big family?

Where would they meet? What would they talk about? What would they do?

The world *is* one big family. The name of that family is the United Nations. Sometimes it is called the UN for short.

The UN was started on October 24, 1945. World War II had just ended. Millions of people had died and suffered in that war. The countries that started the UN wanted to work together to stop wars from happening ever again.

Each year people all over the world celebrate United Nations Day on October 24.

UN Headquarters as seen from the East River. There are five buildings on the 16-acre site: the domed General Assemby building, the tall glass and marble Secretariat, the low rectangular Conference building, the Dag Hammarskjold Library, (not visible here), and South Annex building.

Not all countries belong to the United Nations. But 157 countries do belong. They meet at United Nations Headquarters in New York City.

The United Nations flag has a map of the world as seen from the North Pole. It was adopted by the General Assembly in 1946. This official seal appears on official documents and UN publications.

The United Nations flag is blue and white. In the center is a map of the world. Around the map is a wreath of olive branches. Olive branches are a sign of peace.

SIX MAIN PARTS

The United Nations is divided into six main parts. These are:

- the General Assembly
- the Security Council
- the Secretariat
- the International Court of Justice
- the Trusteeship Council
- the Economic and Social Council

Many other groups work with these six main parts.

All the countries in the UN belong to the General Assembly. Each country may send five delegates and five alternate delegates. It may also send as many advisers as it wants. But each country—no matter how big or how small—gets only one vote.

The General Assembly meets once a year in

United Nations General Assembly

September. The meetings
last about three months. If
something very important
happens in the world, it
may have a special
meeting.

UN Headquarters, in New York, showing the General Assembly building and the 39-story Secretariat. The flags of UN Member States fly in alphabetical order in a colorful row along the entrance to the grounds.

At its meetings the General Assembly talks about the UN's work. It chooses members for some of the other parts of the UN. It is also in charge of the UN's budget.

Sometimes the General Assembly decides things by voting on them. It may decide that two countries should stop fighting and talk about their problems instead. Or it may decide that another part of the UN should help homeless people in some part of the world.

Then the General Assembly announces what it has decided. But it cannot force countries to

obey any UN decisions.
The General Assembly can
just make suggestions.

The Security Council has
fifteen members. Five
countries are always on it.
They are the People's
Republic of China, France,
the United Kingdom, Russia,
and the United States.

The other ten countries
are elected by the General
Assembly. They stay on
the council for two years.

The fifteen-member Security Council discusses problems between countries.

Each country on the Security Council may send one delegate to its meetings.

The Security Council's main job is to keep peace in the world. Its members must be ready to meet

whenever there is a
problem about peace.

The Security Council
looks at arguments
between countries. It thinks
of ways to settle them. It
may tell UN members to
stop trading with a country
that is behaving badly. It
may even ask UN members
to send military forces to
help stop fighting.

The Security Council
makes its decisions by
voting. All UN members

are supposed to do what the Security Council decides.

The Secretariat takes care of the UN's regular business. The Secretary-General is in charge of the Secretariat.

Members of UN Secretariat stand outside the entrance to the General Assembly building in New York City. Almost 20,000 people work for the organization around the world. Many languages are heard in the UN, but the six official languages are Arabic, Chinese, English, French, Russian, and Spanish.

Above: Former UN Secretary-General
Kurt Waldheim of Austria
Right: UN Secretary-General
Javier Pérez de Cuéllar of Peru

Each year the Secretary-General reports on what the UN is doing. The Secretary-General sets up the Security Council meetings. Thousands of people work in this department.

The Security Council names a person to be Secretary-General. Then the General Assembly votes.

The International Court of Justice is made up of fifteen judges. The Security Council and the General Assembly choose them. Each must be from a different country. Each serves for nine years.

Two views of the International Court of Justice.
The court is located in The Hague in The Netherlands.

Countries that belong to the United Nations may take their legal problems to the International Court of Justice. Sometimes even countries that don't belong may do it. But all countries that go before the court must promise to do what the judges decide.

The Trusteeship Council was formed to help countries that didn't have their own governments. In 1945 there were eleven such countries. They were called trust territories.

The Trusteeship Council chose UN members to govern each of those countries. The governing countries were called trustees. The UN made sure they did a good job of governing.

The Trusteeship Council has helped guide ten territories in Africa and the Pacific to self-government, or independence.

Now ten of the trust territories have their own governments. Only one does not. It is the Trust Territory of the Pacific Islands. The United States is its trustee.

The Economic and Social Council is concerned with making a better life for the hundreds of millions of people plagued by hunger, disease, poverty, and ignorance.

The Economic and Social Council helps people all over the world live a better life. Twenty-seven countries belong to this council. The General Assembly elects them.

The Economic and
Social Council works for
better health in the world.
It asks countries to help
one another with education,
art, and music. It also tries
to help everyone—including
children—obtain the rights
they should have.

SPECIAL AGENCIES

Some special groups work with the UN. They are called agencies. The Economic and Social Council helps these agencies and the UN work together.

One agency, the World Bank, lends money to countries that are trying to grow. The countries can use the money to build dams, railroads, and other improvements.

The Food and Agricultural Organization
helps farmers in Sri Lanka (above)
and Ecuador (left) improve their crops.

The Food and Agricultural Organization (FAO) helps countries with their farms, forests, and fishing waters. Often it sends experts and machinery.

A mobile team, composed of a doctor and a
specialized community health helper,
visits an African village.

The World Health
Organization (WHO) helps
people everywhere live
healthier lives.

Tooth decay still tops the list as the most widespread disease in the world today. WHO sends dentists to villages to help the people (above). The WHO community health worker brings medical care to isolated areas (below).

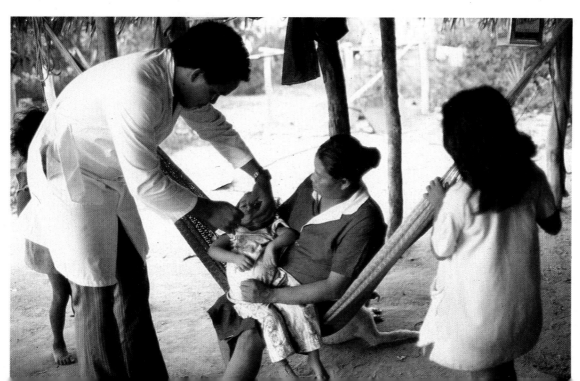

Classroom in Sri Lanka (above). Education is very important in
this island nation.
Village women (below) in Pakistan learn carpet weaving
at the UN sponsored training center.

A rural school near Islamabad in Pakistan.

UNESCO (United Nations Educational, Scientific, and Cultural Organization) works with education, science, and the arts. It helps countries to understand one another better.

The International Labor Organization (ILO) helps workers. It wants the people they work for to treat the workers fairly. And it wants them to live in good homes.

Other special agencies work with the mail, the weather, shipping, air travel, trade, copyrights, and communications.

Children playing in Saxon Gardens in Warsaw, Poland

ESPECIALLY FOR CHILDREN

The part of the United Nations that most children know about is UNICEF. That stands for the United Nations Children's Fund.

UNICEF started in 1946 to help children who had suffered in World War II. Now it helps children everywhere.

Children help UNICEF, too. Many of them collect money by trick-or-treating for UNICEF on Halloween. Some draw pictures for UNICEF greeting cards. Some buy presents at UNICEF shops.

Many children collect money for UNICEF on Halloween.

In these ways children earn several million dollars for UNICEF every year.

Governments also give money to UNICEF. With all this money UNICEF sends food and vitamins to starving children. It buys

Mexican children (above) and an
Inca Indian girl from Peru (right)

medicine for sick children.
It hires teachers for
children who have no
schools. It helps homeless
children find places to live.

In 1980 UNICEF spent
$313 million helping

Children from Tibet

children. But it was not enough. Children are still sick, homeless, and dying all over the world.

If you want to help, write: U. S. Committee for UNICEF, 331 East 38th Street, New York, NY 10016.

They'll tell you what you can do.

WORKING TOGETHER

The UN has its own constitution. It is called the charter of the United Nations. The charter tells about the parts of the UN. It lists the rules UN members should follow.

On June 26, 1945, President Harry S. Truman watched as Secretary of State Edward R. Stettinius signed the UN Charter for the United States.

The charter also lists the UN's four purposes:

- to work for peace and safety in the world
- to help nations behave fairly to each other
- to help nations work together to solve their problems
- to be a place where nations can meet and work toward these goals.

Since it was formed, the UN has done a lot to make these things happen.

Women work on a road-building project in Sri Lanka.

The UN also tries to stop countries from making too many nuclear weapons. It asks them to explore and use outer space only for peaceful reasons. It asks them to use the bottom of the sea peacefully, too.

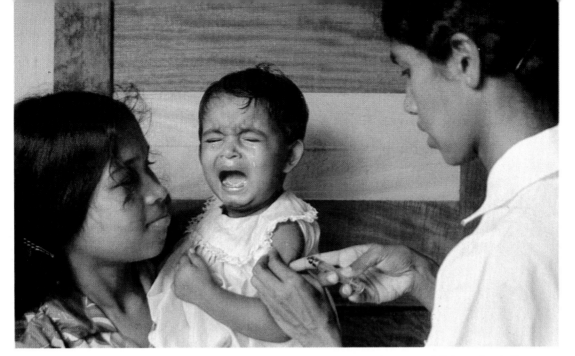
Health care worker innoculates a child against disease.

The United Nations is a world family. Like other families, it has problems. Some of its members don't always do what they should. Some don't keep the peace. Some don't pay their share of expenses.

UN MEMBERS AND THE YEARS IN WHICH THEY BECAME MEMBERS

Afghanistan	1946	Ghana	1957	Philippines	1945
Albania	1955	Greece	1945	Poland	1945
Algeria	1962	Grenada	1974	Portugal	1955
Angola	1976	Guatemala	1945		
Antigua and Barbuda	1981	Guinea	1958	Qatar	1971
Argentina	1945	Guinea-Bissau	1974		
Australia	1945	Guyana	1966	Romania	1955
Austria	1955			Rwanda	1962
		Haiti	1945		
Bahamas	1973	Honduras	1945	Saint Lucia	1979
Bahrain	1971	Hungary	1955	Saint Vincent and the	
Bangladesh	1974			Grenadines	1980
Barbados	1966	Iceland	1946	Sao Tome e Principe	1975
Belgium	1945	India	1945	Saudi Arabia	1945
Belize	1981	Indonesia	1950	Senegal	1960
Benin	1960	Iran	1945	Seychelles	1976
Bhutan	1971	Iraq	1945	Sierra Leone	1961
Bolivia	1945	Ireland	1955	Singapore	1965
Botswana	1966	Israel	1949	Solomon Islands	1978
Brazil	1945	Italy	1955	Somalia	1960
Bulgaria	1955	Ivory Coast	1960	South Africa	1945
Burma	1948			Spain	1955
Burundi	1962	Jamaica	1962	Sri Lanka	1955
Byelorussia	1945	Japan	1956	Sudan	1956
		Jordan	1955	Suriname	1975
Cambodia (Kampuchea)	1955			Swaziland	1968
Cameroon	1960	Kenya	1963	Sweden	1946
Canada	1945	Kuwait	1963	Syria	1945
Cape Verde	1975				
Central African Republic	1960	Laos	1955	Tanzania	1961
Chad	1960	Lebanon	1945	Thailand	1946
Chile	1945	Lesotho	1966	Togo	1960
China	1945	Liberia	1945	Trinidad & Tobago	1962
Colombia	1945	Libya	1955	Tunisia	1956
Comoros	1975	Luxembourg	1945	Turkey	1945
Congo	1960				
Costa Rica	1945	Madagascar (Malagasy)	1960	Uganda	1962
Cuba	1945	Malawi	1964	Ukraine	1945
Cyprus	1960	Malaysia	1957	USSR (Russia)	1945
Czechoslovakia	1945	Maldives	1965	United Arab Emirates	1971
		Mali	1960	United Kingdom	1945
Denmark	1945	Malta	1964	United States	1945
Djibouti	1977	Mauritania	1961	Upper Volta	1960
Dominican Republic	1945	Mauritius	1968	Uruguay	1945
		Mexico	1945		
Ecuador	1945	Mongolia	1961	Vanuatu	1981
Egypt	1945	Morocco	1956	Venezuela	1945
El Salvador	1945	Mozambique	1975	Vietnam	1977
Equatorial Guinea	1968				
Ethiopia	1945	Nepal	1955	Western Samoa	1976
		Netherlands	1945		
Fiji	1970	New Zealand	1945	Yemen	1947
Finland	1955	Nicaragua	1945	Yemen, South	1967
France	1945	Niger	1960	Yugoslavia	1945
		Nigeria	1960		
Gabon	1960	Norway	1945	Zaire	1960
Gambia	1965	Oman	1971	Zambia	1964
Germany, East	1973	Pakistan	1947	Zimbabwe	1980
Germany, West	1973	Panama	1945		
		Papua New Guinea	1975		
		Paraguay	1945		
		Peru	1945		

But all of the member countries know they need their UN family. They need it to keep the peace. They need it for help when they're in trouble. So, in spite of their problems, they go on trying to work together in the United Nations.

The UN works for world peace. This statue by the Russian sculptor,
Yevgeny Vuchetich, was given to the UN by the Soviet Union. It shows
a man beating the sword of war into a plowshare, a farming tool
used here as a symbol of peace.

Young dancers from Nairobi, Kenya.

If you would like to write to the United Nations, here is its address: Office of Public Information, United Nations Headquarters, New York, NY 10017.

WORDS YOU SHOULD KNOW

advisers(ad •VIZE • erz) — people who can tell others how to do
   something in the best way

agency(A •jen • cee) — a group of people acting for other people
   and working toward goals of one type

assembly(ah •SEM • blee) — a gathering together of people for a
   purpose

budget(BUJ • et) — a plan for spending money

charter(CHAR •ter) — a written agreement

communication(kah • myoon • ih •KAY • shun) — ways
   information is exchanged between people
   through written, oral, or physical messages

copyright(COP • ee • rite) — legal right to make and sell materials
   of a written, musical, or artistic nature

council(COWN • sil) — a group of people who meet for discussion
   and advice on certain matters

decisions(dih •SIZH • unz) — solutions, conclusions

delegate(DEL • ih •get) — a person chosen to act for others at
   meetings

department(dih •PART • ment) — a part of a whole, a section of
   an organization

experts(X •perts) — persons who have special skills or information

goals(GOLES) — ends toward which people work

government(GUV •ern • ment) — the group of people who rule
   and make decisions for a country

headquarters(HED • kwor • terz) — the place where meetings and
   discussions for an organization take place

judges(JUJ • iz) — officials elected or named by others to decide
   on questions of law

rights(RITES) — something that everybody should expect, for
   instance, the right to life

trade(TRAYDE) — the exchange of goods and services

vote(VOHT) — to express a decision for or against something

INDEX

About the Author

Carol Greene has written over 25 books for children, plus stories, poems, songs, and filmstrips. She has also worked as a children's editor and a teacher of writing for children. She received a B.A. in English Literature from Park College, Parkville, Missouri, and an M.A. in Musicology from Indiana University. Ms. Greene lives in St. Louis, Missouri. When she isn't writing, she likes to read, travel, sing, do volunteer work at her church—and write some more. Her The Super Snoops and the Missing Sleepers *and* Sandra Day O'Connor, First Woman on the Supreme Court *have also been published by Childrens Press.*